Little Human Things

poems
Sarah A. Etlinger

Clare Songbirds Publishing House Poetry Series
ISBN 978-1-947653-86-3
Clare Songbirds Publishing House
Little Human Things© 2020 Sarah A. Etlinger

All Rights Reserved. Permission to reprint individual poems must be obtained from the author who owns the copyright.

Printed in the United States of America
FIRST EDITION

Clare Songbirds Publishing House Mission Statement:
Clare Songbirds Publishing House was established to provide a print forum for the creation of limited edition, fine art from poets and writers, both established and emerging. We strive to reignite and continue a tradition of quality, accessible literary arts to the national and international community of writers, and readers. Chapbook manuscripts are carefully chosen for their ability to propel the expansion of art and ideas in literary form. We provide an accessible way to promote the art of words in order to resonate with, and impact, readers not yet familiar with the siren song of poets and writers. Clare Songbirds Publishing House espouses a singular cultural development where poetry creates community and becomes commonplace in public places.

140 Cottage Street
Auburn, New York 13021
www.claresongbirdspub.com

Contents

Little Human Things	7
Overwhelming Concerns	8
Peaches for Lunch	10
Reflections on Narcissus	11
In Which We Discuss W.S. Merwin and I Become a Thief	12
The Pope's Whites	14
Eve Eavesdrops on Adam's Conversation with God, After the Fall	15
In Love Everything Looks Like a Metaphor	16
The Timekeeper	17
If I Had Come with You to the Soccer Game in the Rain, I Would Have Brought Coffee	20
Thank Goodness for the Poets	21
Plymouth Rock (Or, A History Lesson)	22
Gematriyot	24
Lavoisier's Law	25
Swimming Lesson	26
What the Pope Said	28
Sometimes I Still Dream of Heaven	29
Study in Pink	30
Transubstantiation	31
Pieta (Reimagined)	32
Playing with Fire	35
Only a Translation	36
My Heart Prepares for Winter on an Autumn Morning	39

The author wishes to thank the following publications for originally printing the works that appear in this book.

"Overwhelming Concerns" appeared in *Vessel Press* October, 2018.

"Reflections on Narcissus" appeared in *Ghost City Review*, October 2018.

"Playing with Fire" appeared in *Neologism Poetry Journal*, September 2018.

"Gematriyot", "Transubstantiation," and "What the Pope Said" appeared in *The Amethyst Review* (Sept 22, Oct 19, and Oct 31, respectively).

"In Which We Discuss W. S. Merwin and I Become a Thief" appeared in *Brine*, Issue 2, January 2019.

"Thank Goodness for the Poets" appeared in *Mookychick*, January 2019.

"The Timekeeper" appeared in *Twist in Time Literary Magazine*, Spring 2019.

"Peaches for Lunch" appeared in *Pink Plastic House—a Tiny Journal*, April 19, 2019.

for Kevin—thank you for your (nearly) two decades of friendship and wisdom.

Little Human Things

Sometimes, when it rains,
I wish I could breathe you in:
rain makes me believe in God
and in the puddles of time
where we would become
a curl of neck and hair,
of breath and skin,
and traces on your face
left by raindrops—

we would be miracles and marvels,
caught like dewdrops
in a spider web, trembling
as gentle breezes haunt trees

we would be freckles in the sun,
kisses of salt from the sea,
fingers holding the grass
so we wouldn't slide away
back into the sky's hold—

you and I tucked together
soft, silent, delicate as frost's creep
on windowpanes
would be the miracle
they write about in books,
along with all the other little human things

we discuss in the dark,
and that ration out the days
we do not possess.

Overwhelming Concerns

Whatever do we call
an abundance of memory
but an absence of sleep

or the pattern left on my sheets
(that has not yet vanished)
by your sleeping body?

What is the name
for the precise movements
between silences,

through imaginary
eons in breath, the angles
of dark and light

that shape the sky
out beyond your reach
on my own body?

What do we call the tools
that would help us measure
the way your voice fills the air

or the lovely curve your hair
makes across your forehead,
half-sticky but so smooth?

What do we call
the things we can't have
but our bodies know,

breathe them, our cells
produce them,
those things the enzymes

combine to make chemicals
evolved just to tell
you their names?
Whatever do we call
the gathering of sighs
or the kinetic hopes of fingers,
the potential caresses
haunting the spaces in night
where only we vibrate

or grow out of the earth like blades
sharpened by alluvial journeys
but smooth when spread out

together, comforting and earthy
a blanket for a picnic?

Peaches for Lunch

One turn of the wheel
and it's high summer in full bloom,
the warm saffron sun painting names
on rocks and grass;
and suddenly there we are,
dropped into this luminous tableau,
the breeze laughing the curls out of my hair
and your eyes into smiles, and we run
through the high grass with bare feet,
toes kissing the cool dark earth—
you pull on my arm, as if pulling the day
longer and longer like the hours of solstice,
and we breathe in the proud poppies
and all that warm green;

and we hoped and believed and wished
we could live in love like this always
and we sat high on the hill to eat peaches for lunch,
their golden pulp oozed into the sky
and the whole world warm before us
and there we were again,
glistening with droplets from floating naked
in the water's hug and maybe,
maybe you were happy
because you said
let's plant the peach pits
so they'll grow into a tree.

Reflections on Narcissus

The vase of daffodils you gave me
sits on the center table,
aching yellow and preening
atop hollow tubes cut
precisely at the knees
to be top heavy and glorious.

They hold the air hostage:
I cannot help but think
of Narcissus, forced to endure
his own reflection for eternity;
condemned to draw nutrients
from clear water.
But when I look at them all,
fanned out, their stems
hugged together in the clearest water,
I realize:

sometimes the body chooses hollow—
chooses water
or a patch of snow outside
rather than early spring soil
full of richness;

sometimes the fear
of not drowning remains
more powerful
than that which could save us.

In Which We Discuss W.S. Merwin and I Become a Thief

I.
The angles of your voice
slid into slow geometry,
lengthy as the afternoon haze
that crept into your hair—
your syllables heavy
with the heat
and the dark gestures
waving across your forehead—

as we talked about Merwin.

II.
I leaned against your car,
watching the heat seep
into the pores of the afternoon
and the blue-dew satin blink
of your eyes as you told me
about the shape of Merwin's soul:
deep and wide,
hollowed out by the sadness
that drowned him
(you have never been so hopeful as I)—

but I do not think this is true,
for I take instruction in Merwin's commands:

in "Beginning," Merwin implores,
"Bring your nights with you"—
and I think he means
come as you are, bring everything
you ever held close and feared
packed in a black suitcase
lined with neatly folded squares
of guilt and padded with the grease
of dried tears—

or perhaps he means
bring your nights with you
so you can lie with me,
languorous as the summer afternoon,
drowning in the waves of my touch
on your body;
the call, like hungry seagulls,
of my kiss pecking your flesh—

bring your nights with you
so we can dip, naked
as emergent butterflies
with droplets on their wings—
into the gentle ocean
of our dreams,
where all is healed and new
in the baptismal water of caress,
in the beautiful shape of sleep.

III.
The heat hung above us like power lines
and you turned to me
with your quiet, magnetic look.

I saw the shape of your soul,
a quick, quivering blip
flickering among the sinewaves—

I reached for it, grabbed it,
and put it in my purse
before you noticed.

The Pope's Whites

You had dreams of stained glass
and the sweetest holy water
in your eyes
every time you looked at me.

But that church closed,
ages ago—trapping
the ghosts and faint
traces from ceremonial flowers,
as if the saints themselves
held them in bouquets
for eternity
as they waited
to meet God.

The truth is, dearest,
the Pope's harsh white
is a lie:

angels do his laundry
on wispy washboards
made from clouds
while he waits, staring
at the dirty water,
praying that the stains will come out.

Eve Eavesdrops on Adam's Conversation with God, After the Fall

God asked Adam,
"How are the apples?"
to which Adam replied,
"I haven't tried any yet, Abba."
But God could smell earth
on his skin and sweet succor
on his breath; he said
"Why do you lie to me, my son?"

Eve, eavesdropping,
would have just said,
"The apples were delicious"
or "One or two were mealy"
or "They made a lovely pie"
or even "When I bit into it, I found a worm."

Now she swallows her punishment
in jagged, crunchy lumps;
and her cells grow
protection around it. The red, red
skin, gilded with sunlight still
tastes like sweet earth,
and she relishes.

Adam, for his shame,
will never get to taste this.

In Love Everything Looks like a Metaphor

I come from the land of beautiful goddesses,
your body my only temple.
I learn its invisible rhythms as waves learn the shore.

Your feather fingers coax my skin to velvet petals;
my arms are branches sore from newness.
I become a fern, verdant and coiled in the earth at your
feet.

The alchemy of your breath on my neck
transforms into ghosts: your sleep-sigh carries remnants of
April.

Mornings in bed with you taste like rivers
full of fresh spring rain. I dive into the deltas
in your eyes, where myths grow.
I swim in the rooms of your broken heart.

The sun through the window shines a lament:
you turn into wind, then light through the trees
in the sky to diamonds.

Hours morph into cups of sugar.
Time is a green shard of sea glass I tuck in my pocket.

I tell you I will hold you as rocks contain water,
and I will write every poem your skin holds.

You say, *everything has limits.*

The Timekeeper

You kept time
beads in a drawer
that you showed me
the first time we met.
You pulled it open
and there they were,
nearly vibrating, encased
in the velvet arms of the drawer
like so many millions
of porcelain eyes.

Amidst a handful of morning light
through the window
you placed one on my bare chest
and I felt the day
lengthen like dough:
translucent, taut,
(so much like the skin
on your neck I can still taste
only springing back
into place when I touched it).

Sometimes even without you
I would feel a tightening
in my throat
or the quickening of heartbeat:
you were speeding up time again—
the sky would move
as if on rollerskates above me
and I'd feel the shrink
and suction in my cells.

Sometimes you kept a few beads
in your wallet
(for Neruda—*Neruda when I want to remember,
you said*)
and you would take them out,

one by one, rolling them
between your moonbeam fingers,
enjoying their glassy texture
as they slowly tumbled and bowled
on your skin.
Often, you would shave a bead down precisely:
(10 minutes here, 78 seconds there;
carve out an extra hour
or cut 16 minutes off our drive)
and I would find little curls
in the vacuum bag
or next to your plate
or in the front seat of a friend's car—
and I knew you had been trying
to find more time or less time.

And once you handed me
a bead and said:
here is an extra hour
let's go have fun
so we spent the hour
like children,
putting hotdogs in strangers' pockets
and, later, we giggled
while we made love
outside on the grass—
three more beads
against the curtain
of sunshine on the water.

Once, you put a bead
between your teeth
and crushed it into shards
that dissolved as they scattered.
Then you said we were free:
you had finally
found a way
to make it stop.

Instead, I said, Maybe
invisible pieces hang on
to our skin;
maybe we keep
the molecules with us
as time dissipates into the air,
and we breathe it in.

If I Had Come with You to the Soccer Game in the Rain, I Would Have Brought Coffee

in a thermos. We would have come from making love
just as the clouds whispered into place;
quiet as the morning, smiles on our skin,
tender as spring rain.

We would sit on zinc bleachers shellacked
by rain, huddled together under your umbrella,
exchanging the shy, knowing smiles
of lovers thick in the parabola of a new relationship—
where marvels grow on trees for us to pluck
and show each other, where routines
become new maps to chart
and where we are both explorers.

At your shiver, I would hand you the thermos
I had tucked in my bag. You would drink, slowly,
from its cup, your eyes glancing at me,
admiring my thoughtfulness. "I never would have thought
to bring this," you would say;
I would shrug and nuzzle your neck.

Only later would I feel the weight
while I washed the lunch dishes
at your house. The next rainy soccer game,
you would nestle the thermos
among your wallet and keys,
mundane as Wednesday. You would remember
I did this, and you would continue
this ritual, now, without me,
though my traces would always remain.

You would hook behind me, your nose
charting the lines of my neck, once again
tender, love seeping away
through the cracks of the air.
I would not return your embrace:
I would only feel my own erasure.

Thank Goodness for the Poets

They're the ones
who can help you find
streams and rivers of green
in the sunlight or a crisp ridge
of opal at the moment the wine hits
your throat to warm it

and they'll tell you how a crack
looks like the sound of leaves
crunched on a sidewalk
or that a teapot whistling
recalls the taste of spring

and they will tell you
that maybe your best color
is vanity
(and perhaps maybe after all
you *could* wear it just a little more
but only on the weekends)
because it flushes your cheeks
so beautifully.

Yes, thank goodness for the poets

because without them
there would be no you and I
to dance in the whispers
dusk leaves on our pillows;
whose kisses birds echo
as they forgive the night
and greet the day
from auspicious branches.

Plymouth Rock (Or, A History Lesson)

You told me once that your mother's family
traced her ancestors back to the Mayflower.
Your people came to a new place,
killed off the natives,
and coaxed the land to give
them all it had, even when it fought back.
They took the rocks and sand,
the hulls of lobster shells
scattered in a marine graveyard,
and bones of the dead
that had been there for all those years,
after storms and diseases and colonizers' mutinies
and buried them
under only a blessing.

I, too, have journeyed here in search of roots.
When I look at Plymouth Rock,
I see the outline of your face
I would learn with my fingers,
and re-learn, again and again
and again with my breath,
even and measured, regular
as the pendulous tide
stretching out now before me.

The Pilgrims had learning to do, too:
how to live upon that wild craggy shore,
huddling in makeshift huts
as snow descended, wild as ocean
winds and cold as bones.
But the Pilgrims prevailed,
believing as they did
that this land was foretold,
that this was divine Providence,
that this was for them
to shape and mold.

Your link, your connection to the Pilgrims
all makes sense now:
it is in your blood,
the very fibers of your body
and in the jelly of your cells,
to stake your claim,
re-write the threads of history,
invade memories and bodies
that weren't yours in the first place.

As the rock rests there in deep slumber
tucked in the sand,
I imagine it dreams of determined feet
marching across its humped back
to tame wild lands—
but I am not a Pilgrim and I am not a patriot.

Alone, now, as I lean over the cold
iron railings, the scent of seaweed
rising between the slats,
it all makes sense.

Gematriyot

All those old Kabbalists
sitting in dark rooms, with
mystical abaci
counting and pacing and
counting some more, spin meaning
to fit each letter, so,
when called, they are filled with
sorcery: ordering
the universe bit by bit,
pattern by pattern,
shamanistic wallpaper
for the rooms in our brains.

As planes and syllables
slide along their axes
especially in your voice,
I cannot help but hear them
there, commanding
the letters to line up
and march, but some refuse:

some let go of the neat
arrangement and careen on echoes,
rejecting the order of the world,
spilling out.

This is what my rabbi
means, I think, when he says
some things are just not ordained.

Gematriyot (or gematria) is a Jewish version of numerology, where each character is assigned a number and, when "added" up, the numbers can be said to have a particular meaning. However, this is not a traditional practice, as it is found in the Kabbalah—books of Jewish mysticism.

Lavoisier's Law

I think of all the things
you wanted me to know:
your son's first word,
his brother's memory of pancakes on Saturday mornings,
why you wear contacts and when,
that time you said you were naked
in bed on the day you stayed home from work;
that you can feel vibrations
deep down in your pores
(maybe even in your cells).

I have my own tokens, too:
the morning sun in your eyes
making prisms in mine,
the scent of your hair after lovemaking,
the memory of my lips on your forehead;
sometimes I even hear
a cadence or two of your voice
in the staccato of birdsong—
all this woven into the fabric
of my days, of my body
like spare string tucked
among twigs in a nest.

But these forms you left have shifted,
vanished into the air:
you will come down as rain
and touch my face again
or maybe someone else
is breathing you now—
even as you walk to your car
holding her hand, filling her shape;
you are not the same as you were.

We are not simply
the sum of all parts:
there are always things that spill over,
ooze out of cracks
in hot pavement and evaporate.

Swimming Lesson

Once again July at Lake Sunapee
and the horizon has fallen
into the green serrations of eastern pines;

and, small as hiccups of breeze on the water,
there we are:
you, giddy from sunbathing
and exuberant calls after loons—and I,
treading water like a humming motor;
you reach for me, try to pull me close,
but I resist: I want to swim across the lake,
my head bobbing along the buoys,
feet still visible in the sepia water.

I grew up swimming in the ocean
and I would let the waves break
across my young body, shatter against me,
until I reached the place
beyond the breaks where the water, green and calm,
sighed along with the wind
and my father and I would float,
happy and peaceful,
the taste of youth still in my mouth,
hair greased by salt and surf.

But you do not have water in your veins
or the ocean in your bones.
You do not understand how,
even when waves can no longer crack along my body,
I want to swim past the silent paths
of ducks and loons, to where
the rocks click as they border the shore,
where the light cannot find
my gliding feet as my toes stretch the water thin.

No, you cannot know why
the tide pulls me out—
as I look toward the shore,
where you're watching me.
I turn, reach my arm out of the water,
carefully straighten the horizon.

What the Pope Said

Your beautiful creases
spread on mine like breath
on a windowpane:
invisible except
in the right conditions
of temperature and light.

At night, I glow in the dark:
indelible patterns
from your breath
inked into my flesh,
the living map
of where we've been.

The pope has said
that hell doesn't exist—
souls only disappear.

Sometimes I Still Dream of Heaven

I opened up my dream
and there you were, soft
as love's velvet, and my kisses
were violets, fresh new purple
offering dew to hang around
our necks. I held a marble of sky
in my palm, planted seeds of clouds
along the soft taper of your hips,
and rain fell around us like a skirt
keeping us dry. When the sun came out
it was rosy, nostalgic: now only the sky
remembered, but I could taste you
everywhere.
       Then, your eyes held dreams
like pearls: Heaven, contained.
Everything that needed to be said
was in your voice.

Study in Pink

I ran too fast
across the sand shimmering
with pink kisses
to meet you—

to feel your arms lift me
to zero gravity—

when we and the sun and the sand and the sky—
cut only by the heavy hem of water—

shared the same hue

Transubstantiation

Whenever a Jewish woman is pregnant,
it's believed, she could carry the Messiah.
Maybe that's why she can't help but feed you.
How like Mary: preparing a hidden feast
for your belly like the nourishment
growing in hers, perfect conditions
for growing a life.

Maybe that's why I take
such pleasure in feeding you—
they say the spirit resides
in pieces of barren cracker
and in the sweetness of wine;
Jews do not believe this, and yet
my holy ancestor
crawls out of hiding when we're alone
and I'm praying the rosary on your chest:
each rib a mystery
       (Oh hail those holy mysteries
         as your heart beats…)

each beat *hail my holy Queen*
my life my sweetness my hope
oh hail hail my holy Queen

each breath a decade
each "Glory Be" my kiss—

You make Mother of me
sweetness my hope oh welcome to Grace
you make Mother of me
there on your chest
from the very breaths I grow
within the deepest cells
of my body.

Pieta (Reimagined)

I.
The pews' cold surprises me:
despite the warm amber
of their wooden torsos
(as if they, too, mourn the loss
of this young woman)
their hard laps prop us up.
When the service begins all I can see
is the little girl she left behind;
she wears a black velvet dress
and shiny Mary Janes that squeeze
her still-chubby toddler feet
as they dangle from her grandmother's arms.

Later, my mother asks how I'm doing
and I tell her about the service;
my student, her little girl, her mother.
We are quiet for awhile,
but then she tells me

II.
her name was Becky
and we had homeroom together.
I used to sit with her sometimes.
She would tell me about her weekend.
One Friday she told me
she was going sailing with her dad.
I said, "I think that will be fun"
and she said "Thanks. Maybe you can come next time."
And I said, "Sure."

Monday morning I didn't see her
because we had an assembly
where they told us
"…there has been an accident…"
Becky drowned sailing—
she fell off the boat and couldn't swim
to safety fast enough.

I imagine Becky's voice, a caught fish
in her throat, squirming and thrashing
to release the hook from its tongue,
but the hook holds fast—
and she swallows it, swallows it whole
till it catches in her belly,
the skin growing round to protect it—
until now.

I imagine my mother, too,
small and thin, at her friend's funeral
in awkward clothes,
buttressed in familiar pews
before she walks up to the coffin.
Though it is cool, white—
an oyster of death—
it feels warm to her touch;
her first lesson in death:
it is not so cold.

III.
As we talk about the funeral
my mother says she wants to be cremated
and scattered in the lake.
I will try. You don't want an urn for the ashes? I joke.
No. I never understood that—
my mother used to wear ashes around her neck all the time.
I can almost see my grandmother
wearing a silver vial, suspended
between her breasts by a thick silver chain;
last traces encased by sandy glass
and kept close to her heart.

But the earth keeps fossils as relics, too:
water worries rock and shells
to sand, to dust
as the priest calls
"Remember you are dust and to dust you shall return"
on Ash Wednesday as he paints ashes
on the forehead.

I can see all these mothers, now,
trying to balance the weight of the present
on arms burdened by ghosts.

IV.
As I leave the church
and stand on the steps,
there's the statue of Mary,
her face placid, calm, accepting;
her weathered granite hands
stretch out for mine.
I reach for her, take her finger,
and grasp.

Playing with Fire

You reached up with your tongue to grab a star,
holding it like a throbbing marble
between your lips—
as we kissed, its traces
filled my throat so I could
swallow its light whole
like a lump of mercury

before you placed it, still humming,
on your wrist, where I could almost see
the silver lining through your veins—
under the skin a slow heavy drip—twisting
droplets to slick our bodies
into quivering nebulas

then
at the very moment God's lightning hand
reached down through the summer light
full of fireflies
you moved the star to my chest
before it dissolved
into a glittering éclat of memory.

Only a Translation

This is only a translation
of a feeling, a look—
of sand remnants between my toes
and of you—

you and your sideways smiles
broken only by cracked memories;
your clumsy feet finding measures
of ground, never enough
and probably not
thwarted by pebbles;

your jittery posture
moving through space;
your own memories
spilling into mine, bleeding
into prisms of light and pigment
the way watercolors spread
across canvases at the museum

where we stood,
hands by our sides,
the minds of our fingers searching
for the other, starved
in the same way we keep trinkets
on shelves or islands trapped
in lockets—to be found,
to be discovered by other fingers,
pulling the sheets of history.

That First Morning

I laced the butter on your toast
with all of your insecurities
and spread a little of the jam I made
from the fruity lumps of your loneliness
garnished with a few dips
from the bag of sighs on the counter.

You were none the wiser,
for you had no idea I kept these things
in jars stored neatly in my heart
next to the scrapbooks full of your sorrows,
their faces grotesque and holy,
wincing and howling like ghosts;
you had no idea how long I've kept them
in the garrets of my eyes
and in the cellars of my voice—

and even on that first morning
when I made you breakfast,
carried the tray to where you still slept,
your back bare and coaxed smooth from love,
I doubted you would ever come to know.

Image by Muklin

My Heart Prepares for Winter on an Autumn Morning

The night's slack has loosened
and morning spills out,
the essence of autumn

flowing in waves. Beyond,
morning has rubbed
the lake to pewter chenille,

corduroy fabric for the seagulls
that cringe and squawk
far above my head. I'm looking

out at the horizon
and I can hear your voice
in the sway of trees;

slowing rhythms choreographed
by weather's invisible baton,
just as your breath would even

out the hours, your soft torso
tucked against the sheets
measuring our dreams.

Everything rushes, now—
squirrels dart this way and that,
birds speckle the cool sky

and a shallow breeze
creaks between the trees
so their leaves, already crackling

with beige and scarlet, begin
to think about what's to come,
their exuberant, inevitable plunge.

Author's Notes

This book is the result of the adage "Just keep writing": I kept writing, and I got another book! But it wasn't so simple as sitting down and scrawling (and crossing out, and re-scrawling, and cutting up). As with raising children, it took an entire village and several states—yes, states!—to see this one to completion. Without the invaluable contributions from some wonderful people, none of us would be reading this page.

Formally, I'd like to thank Laura Williams French and the rest of the staff at Clare Songbirds Publishing house for their work on this beautiful book. Their dedication to their craft certainly shows; without their expertise and drive, this book would simply not be the book it is.

Additionally, my heartfelt gratitude to my reviewers: Dan and Rebecca Hansen, Margaret King, and Mark Wagenaar. Your reviews not only took time out of your busy schedules, but they helped me to gain valuable insight into this collection and illuminated things for me I did not see. Thank you.

To my early (and ongoing) readers—Becky Hansen, Pam Inglese, Lisa Kortebein, Molly Sides—your patience is unmatched. Thank you for allowing me once again to send you many drafts, sometimes messy or unfinished ones, and thank you for your excellent reading of my work. More importantly, thank you for the support and feedback you provide to me (and for not getting angry when I send you the 17th version in a text message or ask you strange, random questions about words).

And to Kathleen Dale, whose mentorship and expert editing skills have been essential to this project and to all of my work: your ability to see a poem's potential, especially when the author does not, is a rare gift. Your keen eye, indefatigable knowledge of grammar, and commitment to coherence will always be greatly appreciated, in addition to your patience. I could not have done this without you, the endless coffee, or even Eliot's vigilance from the stairs. Thank you.

More informally, but no less importantly, I want to thank my personal network of friends and family who always lift me up. First, to my wonderful husband Brad Houston: thank you for spending weekends and evenings with Gabriel so I could write these poems. Even though you're the first to say you don't "do poetry," you certainly do *support* this poet through cheering me on and encouraging me to market my work. Thank you for all you do for me. And to Gabriel for always grounding me, for loving me as his Mama no matter what, and for his amazing gifts for vocabulary. Though I may have made him a reader, he has made me a poet; the many hours we spend reading together rekindled my love for language, beauty, and rhythm.

Thank you to my parents, my sister and her family, and to all of my extended family. Your pride and love for me has been indispensable. I am very grateful I've been able to count on you for always being my cheering squad, no matter what crazy endeavor I set my mind to or where I've wanted to move next. You haven't let the distance diminish your support, and for that I am eternally thankful.

Sincere thanks to my tribe both at work and at home, particularly: Valerie Blair (who, both times around, holds the record for most copies purchased—because you can never have too many books!), Tracy Kruse, Molly Sides, Kevin Wozniak, Liana Odrcic, Gabby Bachhuber, Lisa Woodall, Allison Castillo, Alexis Whyte, Kelly and Peter Baran, Colleen Halverson, Carol Ostrom, Aaron Witham, and Elizabeth Johnston. Your support and love made this all possible and continues to be a source of encouragement as I selfishly cancel plans or scribble during meetings. Thank you for always understanding what it takes to make this work.

Finally, to the one person who does most of the heavy lifting aside from my husband: Martin Quirk. Even for this chatty poet who has opinions and commentary about everything, words fail me when it comes to thanking you enough. Though you don't realize it, all of the miles walked helped me write; all of the conversations helped me to see my potential and grow into it; and—most importantly—to develop an unbreakable bond based on mutual respect and admiration. You may not be a poet or "good with words" (or with commas), but you are an incredible friend whose tireless support continues to amaze me. Not a single word of this would have happened, or be as meaningful, without you. Plus, you're the best nacho companion anyone could ever want. "Thank you" isn't sufficient, but it'll have to do.

Sarah A. Etlinger is an English professor who lives in Milwaukee, WI, with her family. She is also the author of *Never One for Promises* (Kelsay Books, 2018) and a Pushcart and Best of the Net nominee. Her work can be found in places such as *The Amethyst Review, Bramble, Mookychick* and *Neologism Poetry Journal*, among others, and the anthologies *Mansion* and *You are Not Your Rape*. When not writing or teaching, she can be found at the lake, cooking/baking, traveling and learning to play piano.

Look for her at www.sarahetlinger.com, on Facebook, and on Twitter at @drsaephd.

www.ingramcontent.com/pod-product-compliance
Lightning Source LLC
Chambersburg PA
CBHW052128110526
44592CB00013B/1796